HIGH PRAISE FOR BREAKING FORTH 2 DESTINY

Breaking Forth 2 Destiny is a powerfully penned stimulant of a book. It urges and encourages the reader to trust God unequivocally. To know that despite how dire circumstances may appear, God still controls the outcome of our lives. Dr. Williams skillfully guides us through the process of our matriculated development through the prolific examples of Abraham; allowing us to witness him as he trusts God for that which is beyond his comprehension. You will surely benefit from reading about the "friend of God" as his template for 'believing' and his quest for seeking life's purpose coincides so powerfully with many of the same challenges we face today. This is a good book.

The Right Reverend Dr. Matthew M. Odum
Pastor/Teacher, Temple of Glory Community Church
Savannah, Georgia

God has used His vessel, Pastor Brennetta, to pour pavement for a life-changing journey as you travel on the road this book provides. Scholars, clergy, and laity will benefit greatly from this groundbreaking study! While purpose and potential are discussed, I believe they will be clearly magnified and manifested through one vehicle the reader will ride in, and that vehicle of transport is your EXPECTATION of GOD! So, release your expectation… and be blessed by the ride!

Apostle Dr. Rita L. Twiggs
Rita Twiggs Ministries, Inc.

This work is rich, relevant, and restoring! I had pondered and asked many years what I was called to do in life! Without a definitive response, I pursued many avenues still not being fulfilled. If I had this book before my search, there would not have been any question about my destiny! Dr. Brennetta Williams explicitly shares God's principles on your next dimension. You can stop searching now; your answers to reach your purpose are in this book. She has POSITIONED you for DESTINY.

Dr. Angela Corprew-Boyd
National Preacher, Teacher, Author, and Leadership Consultant

Breaking Forth 2 Destiny is a MUST READ! This book is filled with strategies in how to navigate through life's challenges. It teaches you how to overcome obstacles that try to prevent you from fulfilling your God-given assignment. It teaches you how to embrace opposition and see it as a part of your journey. *Breaking Forth 2 Destiny* teaches you how to position yourself as you walk in your purpose. This book will transform your life!

Reverend Linda A. Pratt
Associate Pastor
The Baptist Worship Center Church

Dr. Williams gives an intricate and detailed account of the reasoning, and often, mental anguish that accompanies the journey to one's destiny. Read this book and be encouraged to learn that struggle and conflict are often necessary, and why embracing obedience is key to this life-affirming process.

Dr. Alycia T. Dickens, Nurse Practitioner
Alycia Dickens, DNP, FNP-BC
CAN Community Health

BREAKING FORTH 2 DESTINY

BREAKING FORTH 2 DESTINY

Arising from where you are to where God has destined for you to be

BRENNETTA C. WILLIAMS

Suffolk, Virginia

Breaking Forth 2 Destiny
Arising from where you are to where God has destined you to be.

Copyright © 2021 by Dr. Brennetta C. Williams
All rights reserved.

All rights reserved. This book is protected by the copyright laws of the United States of America. This book may not be copied or reprinted for commercial gain or profit. The use of quotations or occasional page copying for personal or group study is permitted and encouraged. Permission will be granted upon request.

Final Step Publishing, LLC
PO Box 1441
Suffolk, VA 23439
www.finalsteppublishing.com

Soft cover ISBN: 978-1-7349784-3-8

For Worldwide Distribution. Printed in U.S.A.

Dedication

To my loving and precious daughter, Morgan
My amazing sisters, Cassie, Lisa & Movita
May you be inspired to break forth into your greatest destiny.

Acknowledgments

First and foremost, I acknowledge my Lord and Savior Jesus Christ whose grace, guidance, and strength allowed me to accomplish this milestone. Without Him, the completion of this book would not have been possible.

Secondly, I recognize the love and unwavering support of my wonderful family. I am grateful for the many sacrifices of my husband, Floyd. My daughter, Morgan, has been the wind beneath my wings in encouraging me to persevere. You are truly one of my most treasured gifts. My amazing sisters, Cassie and Lisa, have provided tremendous inspiration on this journey. I appreciate you more than words can ever express. A special thank you to my father, John, who has always supported me and taught me the value of prayer. I honor the memory of my late mother, Lonnie Rae, whose love for God inspired me to seek Him in a deeper way. Thank you to all of my loving extended family who mean the world to me.

Thirdly, I wish to express my sincere appreciation to the Impact Worship Center International Church. I am humbled and grateful for the opportunity to serve such an amazing flock. Your prayers, love, and support have blessed me beyond measure.

A heartfelt thank you to my friends and faithful prayer partners who continually undergird me in prayer. You have been instrumental in helping me to break forth in my destiny.

Words cannot express the depth of my gratitude to my Pastor, Bishop Millicent Hunter. You have impacted my life and ministry in such a profound way. Thank you for your remarkable leadership and guidance on my spiritual journey. I honor the memory of my spiritual father, Apostle William Darryl Scott Sr., on whose shoulders I stand. A special thank you to all of my spiritual mentors who have inspired and encouraged me in becoming the "Me" God ordained. You have served an invaluable purpose in my life and I am forever grateful.

CONTENTS

Foreword   13

Introduction   17

CHAPTER 1
Breaking Into Purpose:
    Positioned for Purpose   19

CHAPTER 2
Breaking Out of the Box:
    Step Up, Step Out, and Step Forth   31

CHAPTER 3
Breaking Free from the Past:
    Let Go and Let God   43

CHAPTER 4
Breaking Through the Obstacles:
    The Giants Must Come Down   55

CHAPTER 5
Breaking into Deeper:
    Take the Limits Off   67

CHAPTER 6
Breaking Forth into Greater:
    Quitting is Not an Option   75

Conclusion   91

About the Author   95

FOREWORD

From the moment I met Dr. Brennetta Williams, I knew that she was someone special. She is a woman of extraordinary wisdom and keen insight into the Word of God and how to apply the wisdom of the Word to your life. In this book, she has the courage to delve deeply into the most important questions we all have about life: what is my purpose and why am I here?

Life is a complicated journey and understanding life can be daunting. The first step to understanding life is to know that God has a plan and purpose for each one of us. Dr. Williams presents a biblically sound investigation and scholarly presentation of God's divine assignment for your life. Knowing that God has a plan and purpose for your life must be the beginning of your quest to discover God's plan for you.

Knowing that God has a plan and purpose for your life will help you to understand that obstacles and hindrances do not interfere with that plan, but instead are vehicles to help you grow in faith and trust in God so that you can be about the business of embracing your destiny. Even before you were born, God had a plan for your destiny and the good works you would do to fulfill it. Christians facing difficult situations today can take comfort in knowing that God's promise is not to immediately rescue you from hardship or suffering, but God's plan for you is to… *"cause all things to work together for your good."*

Therefore, God uses challenges and hardship to strengthen your faith in Him so that you can carry out the plan that He has for you. We don't always understand or agree with God's ways, but when you seek wisdom and guidance from God's Word, you will understand that God allows hardship and challenges to build your faith and trust in Him and give you hope.

For I know the plans I have for you, plans to prosper you, and not to harm you, plans to give you hope and a future (Jeremiah 29:11).

Dr. Williams gives us biblical examples of intriguing stories of individuals whose lives were transformed when they were able to see obstacles and opposition as opportunities to grow in their faith and trust in God. In those stories, she helps us to see parallels in our own life so that we can learn from those biblical examples. Dr. Williams will show you how God is constantly at work in your life. Her writing is clear and concise and will give you great insight into your own life as you seek to discover God's plan and purpose for you. It is my prayer that the Spirit of God will direct you as you read this greatly needed book. As you turn these pages, may you learn how to *break free*, *breakthrough* and *break forth* so that you can step out of your comfort zone and embrace your destiny.

Bishop Millicent Hunter
Pastor, The Baptist Worship Center Church

Introduction

We are all on a journey called life. It is a complicated journey that challenges and changes us. One of the greatest challenges we face is embracing and walking in our purpose. God has given each of us a divine assignment. There is something we were uniquely created to do in the earth. We were created on purpose and for a purpose. This journey is pregnant with possibilities and potential.

Many people struggle to discover their real purpose in life. They wrestle with questions like, "why am I here, what was I created to do, or where do I go from here"? Other individuals have come to the realization of their purpose. There is an understanding of who they are and what they are assigned to do. Somehow, they move from season to season without maximizing their potential. They become stuck in neutral and paralyzed into inactivity. Many obstacles can delay us on the way to fulfilling our destiny. Distractions are often the major culprit. Distractions defocus, discourage, and delay us. Our delays don't deny God's plan for our lives.

The objective of this book is to catapult you to your destiny by empowering you to break free, breakthrough, and break forth to greater. You will learn how to break forth to the next level and dimension in your life. Expect to gain greater clarity on your purpose. You will be empowered to step out of your comfort zone and embrace your destiny.

This book will be instrumental in helping you to overcome obstacles that present hinderances to your progress. It will empower you to boldly embrace your destiny as you break forth to your greatest potential.

Chapter 1
Breaking into Purpose: Positioned for Purpose

> And the Lord visited Sarah as he had said, and the Lord did unto Sarah as he had spoken. For Sarah conceived, and bare Abraham a son in his old age, at the set time of which God had spoken to him. And Abraham called the name of his son that was born unto him, whom Sarah bare to him, Isaac. And Abraham circumcised his son Isaac being eight days old, as God had commanded him. And Abraham was an hundred years old, when his son Isaac was born unto him. And Sarah said, God hath made me to laugh, so that all that hear will laugh with me. And she said, Who would have said unto Abraham, that Sarah should have given children suck? for I have born him a son in his old age.
> **Genesis 21:1-7 KJV**

Life is a journey connected by seasons. Seasons are constantly changing. Many people experience breakthrough seasons, yet they fail to break forth into their greater season. Breaking forth means to burst forward with increase or to burst out suddenly. Breaking forth is moving forward to the next level or dimension. Breaking forth positions us to not only survive but to thrive. We were created on purpose for a purpose to be victorious in every area of our lives. Are you walking in victory or are you stuck between breaking through and breaking forth?

Breaking forth allows us to emerge with power. In the spiritual realm, that power is the manifest power of God. The Holy Spirit empowers and equips us to accomplish what we cannot do on our own. He empowers us to break forth with a greater level of power despite our flaws, failures, and limitations. His power is the catalyst that moves us from where we are to where God purposes us to be.

There is a marked difference between breaking through and breaking forth. A breakthrough experience simply deals with an instance or an act of overcoming something. Breaking free and breaking through set us up to break forth.

We must understand God positions us for purpose. It's not by accident or happenstance we are where we are. Nothing happens unless God permits it. He allows us to be in appointed places at appointed times to accomplish His plans. Some of the difficulties we have experienced were designed to develop us for our destiny. God permits us to endure seasons and circumstances to prepare us for a greater purpose.

Genesis 21:1-7 presents an intriguing story of purpose, promise, and possibility. Abraham received divine instructions from the Lord when he was seventy-five years old. God called him out of the land of Ur of the Chaldeans, to go to the Promised Land which God had given him. Abraham received specific promises for his journey. God promised to make him a great nation and that his name would be great. Abraham was divinely positioned for a greater purpose.

He was commanded to leave a familiar place and journey to an unfamiliar place. God had something greater in store for him and his descendants. Abraham was obedient and stepped out on faith. Without faith, it is impossible to please God. There are blessings connected to our obedience. Our yielding to God's plan and purpose positions us to receive the blessings of the Lord. Obedience to His instructions and directions prepares us to be used in a greater capacity for His glory.

It's not just about us! There are times when the blessings of others are connected to our obedience. Someone is waiting on what's locked up on the inside of us. Someone is waiting on our "yes" to the Lord. They are waiting for us to step out of our comfort zones and embrace our purpose. It's time to arise! This is not the season to sit dormant or be complacent. It's time to arise and walk in our God-given purpose. God is calling forth what He has placed in us. You are anointed for this! The anointing on our lives impacts lives. The world has need of what we are carrying. We can't afford to allow any person's breakthrough to be delayed because of our delayed obedience. Partial obedience and delayed obedience are still disobedience.

The Word of God declares faith is the substance of things hoped for and the evidence of things not seen. It takes radical faith to pursue the unknown. Abraham didn't have any evidence of what was ahead of him. All he had was a promise, but he had the faith to pursue that promise. If all you have is a promise from the Lord, that is enough. One word from God can shift your entire life to greater, but you must possess the faith to pursue after it. Pursuing something means to go after; continue on that path; to follow after.

There will always be obstacles or opposition before any great opportunity. Abraham had a great promise but there was a problem. The fact that Abraham's wife, Sarah, was barren presented an obstacle. She was not able to produce children. How could it be possible that he would be the father of many nations if his wife was barren? Every obstacle is just an opportunity for God to get the glory out of the story.

Often, we allow uncertainty and doubt to hinder our blessings. A lack of faith or limited faith limits possibilities. It causes us to doubt what God has already said. There are no limits with God; He is limitless. We have to trust the God of the process even when we don't comprehend the process. The process prepares us to fulfill our purpose.

Abraham continued onto Egypt after he arrived at the Promised Land. He was still pondering the magnitude of the promise. God knew he was struggling with doubt and uncertainty. The omniscient God confirmed the promise again in Genesis 13:14-16. In verse 16 God says, "I will make your offspring as the dust of the earth, so that if anyone could count the dust, then your offspring could be counted." We understand that it is impossible to count the dust. God reaffirmed Abraham was going to have so many descendants that he was not even going to be able to count them.

Abraham was waiting and anticipating the promise as the years went by. He found himself frustrated with the process. Many of us are holding onto promises or holding onto prophetic words that have not yet manifested. We are trusting God to move in a particular area or waiting on the breakthrough. Waiting patiently is not always an easy task. We are an instantaneous culture that desires everything on demand. The reality is process requires patience. Waiting stretches our faith and tests our patience.

Frustration often appears when the answer is delayed. There is a sense of frustration when it doesn't happen when or how we think it should. It becomes necessary to refocus on the promise and not the problem. If God said it, then it shall come to pass. God is not a man, so he does not lie; He is not human, so he does not change His mind. Has He ever spoken and failed to act? Has He ever promised and not carried it through? (Numbers 23:19)

Abraham was frustrated to the point where he started complaining to God about what had not yet happened. He complained about limitations like his age and his wife's inability to produce children. His focus was on the obstacles and not the promised opportunity.

The Word of the Lord came to Abraham a third time. God assured him again that his own son would be his heir. Genesis 15:5 states, "He took him outside and said, "Look up at the sky and count the stars—if indeed you can count them." Then He said to him, 'So shall your offspring be.'" Abraham was in position for his purpose, but he had to wait. He was in the season of in between. He was in between the vision and the victory. We must learn to wait patiently on the manifestation of the promise.

Abraham and Sarah got tired of waiting. When he was eighty-five and his wife was seventy-five, they decided to construct a plan of their own. It is never wise to abort God's plan for our own. We set ourselves up for failure when we attempt to move ahead of God. Sarah came up with a new plan. She decided to "help God out" by loaning her own Egyptian servant, Hagar, to Abraham. Hagar conceived and bore Abraham a son, Ishmael.

Thirteen years go by, and they think that everything is going well. Abraham now has this son. This boy, Ishmael, is running around, and they believe God has fulfilled His promise. This must be the plan. But in Genesis 17, God comes to Abraham again and tells him that he will be a father of many nations, and that Sarah will bear him a son. Abraham laughs as he is now ninety-nine years old. In Genesis 18, when Sarah hears that she will bear a son, she laughs as well. Has God ever promised you anything that made you laugh? Has he ever shown you something that seems absolutely impossible that all you can do is laugh? I'm sure that's how Abraham and Sarah felt. But if God said it, no matter how ridiculous it sounds, believe that He has the power to bring it to pass. Is there anything too hard for God? If He said it, believe it.

Our key text says that God did as He had promised, and Sarah became pregnant by Abraham, and gave birth to a son, Isaac. God will do just what He said He would do. If God gives you a word, just stand on it no matter how long it seems. God does not go back on His word. He honors His word above His name. God is faithful even when we fail. God does not change His mind about us despite our flaws and mistakes.

Every good idea is not a *God* idea...Sometimes we need to **mind our own business** and let God handle the situation.

Abraham and Sarah initially tried to help God out. They came up with their own secondary plan, but God did not tell them that the promise child would come through Hagar. This might have seemed like a good idea, but it was not God's idea. God already had a plan and a purpose. Sarah was the chosen one; it was Sarah's assignment. She may have been delayed, but she wasn't denied. She was still next. She was positioned for the purpose.

We are sometimes like Sarah. How many times have we pushed the override button in favor of our plan and not God's plan? There are times in our lives when we have attempted to handle circumstances without Him. We may have made some bad decisions and gone down the wrong paths. Our impatient efforts resulted in making the situation worse.

We have to be intentional about minding our own business and allowing God to handle His business. Wait on the Lord and be of good courage. Don't get weary in well doing because in due season we are going to reap if we faint not. God's plan is the best plan. The Bible declares that we should not lean to our own understanding but in all our ways acknowledge Him. He has promised to direct our paths.

Moving ahead of God's timing prematurely sets us up for failure. We will be in the right position at the right time when we wait on the Lord. He knows what's best and when to manifest the promise. Our assignment is to trust God while we stay positioned for purpose.

> God is faithful even when we fail. God does not change His mind about us despite our flaws and mistakes.

Chapter 2
Breaking Out of the Box:
Step Up, Step Out, and Step Forth

> Then they reached Jericho, and as Jesus and his disciples left town, a large crowd followed him. A blind beggar named Bartimaeus (son of Timaeus) was sitting beside the road. When Bartimaeus heard that Jesus of Nazareth was nearby, he began to shout, "Jesus, Son of David, have mercy on me!" "Be quiet!" many of the people yelled at him. But he only shouted louder, "Son of David, have mercy on me!" When Jesus heard him, he stopped and said, "Tell him to come here." So they called the blind man. "Cheer up," they said. "Come on, he's calling you!" Bartimaeus threw aside his coat, jumped up, and came to Jesus. "What do you want me to do for you?" Jesus asked. "My Rabbi," the blind man said, "I want to see!" And Jesus said to him, "Go, for your faith has healed you." Instantly the man could see, and he followed Jesus down the road.
> **Mark 10:46-52 (NLT)**

There is greatness locked inside each of us. The key to breaking forth to greater is stepping up, stepping out, and stepping forward. Breaking forth requires breaking out of the locked box. Boxes can be limiting. They hold and contain items in a limited space. Boxes restrict mobility and limit activity.

All of us have an area of limitation. Limitations are restrictive weaknesses or those things that restrict us. Limitations can limit us, but God can conquer every limitation. What is limiting you from reaching your greatest potential?

Sometimes it seems as if we are in a box on our spiritual journey. We can't seem to move forward as we desire. Our progress, growth, and potential is limited by one hindrance after another. The pressures of life frustrate us and cause us to feel trapped by our circumstances. We wrestle with our self-worth and self-sabotaging ideologies. Often, we are imprisoned by our own thoughts of fear, failure, and intimidation. The enemy attempts to keep us in the box by reminding us of our past failures and present flaws. He is on a mission to cause us to doubt what God has already declared about us. It's time to break out of the box! You can do all things through Christ who strengthens. Step up, step out, and step forward to your next season.

In this text, we find Jesus and His disciples leaving Jericho. They are on their way to Jerusalem to celebrate the Passover. This would be Jesus's last trip to Jerusalem. A large crowd is following Him. They have witnessed the miracle working power of Jesus. They have seen the lame walk, the dumb talk, and the blind see. They recognize Jesus as the one that has the power to deliver and set free!

They encountered a blind beggar by the name of Bartimaeus while they were walking down the road with Jesus. The man's name was significant because it was made up of two Greek words that together indicate Bartimaeus was not only blind, but he inherited his blindness from his father. The prefix *Bar* means son or son of. *Temaus* resembles *tuphlos* which means blind man. Bartimaeus was the son of a blind man. There was a condition being passed from one generation to the next generation.

Bartimaeus inherited a condition that impacted his destiny and limited his potential. He was bound by a condition that caused him to be stuck in a circumstance beyond his control. He couldn't fix, change it, or reverse it. He simply learned to live with his limitations. Many of us can identify with living with limitations. There are obstacles that have the potential to limit our progress, success, and ministries. Limitations are not just physical; they can be

> Our family history does not dictate our story. Jesus has the power over every generational attack on our lives. Jesus has the power to set us free so we can move forward.

social, emotional, and spiritual. Many have mastered the art of functioning from a place of dysfunction.

Often times we are challenged with situations beyond our control. Some circumstances are complicated because their origins are generational in nature. Every now and then, situations from our family follow us. We didn't choose the issues, they are not our fault, we don't want them, and we don't even understand them. Many of us are left with generational baggage that needs to be processed and unpacked.

The enemy will attempt to use generational curses, generational illnesses, and generational addictions to defeat us. The negative impact on our families is undeniable. We don't want to see another family member tied up, tangled up, or messed up. We can be different, but we must have a desire to be different.

We don't have to go down the same path; we don't have to fight the same demons. Our family history does not dictate our story. We are not defeated. We are overcomers. We are not just conquerors; we are more than conquerors. Victory comes through Christ Jesus! Jesus has the power over every generational attack on our lives. Jesus has the power to set us free so we can move forward.

The blood of Jesus covers us. I decree and declare every generational curse on your life is broken in Jesus's name. It shall not prevail. No weapon that's formed against you or your family shall prevail.

Bartimaeus's condition looked permanent, but it was really temporary. We may not have physical blindness, but there are some blind spots in all of our lives. We miss some things because of spiritual blindness. We are so focused on what it looks like in the natural that we don't see what God is doing in the spiritual realm. Every now and then, we have to check our vision.

We don't always see what God is showing us. We don't always see ourselves as God sees us. We often miss seeing the obvious signs of the times. *Vision* is the state of being able to see. The more we get in His presence, the more He will reveal to us. God will show us things from His perspective. We will begin to see things we never saw before. We need God to help us to see beyond ourselves and our circumstances.

Bartimaeus was in need of a breakthrough! He couldn't see his way out, but God saw him. God has not forgotten about us. He sees us in the valley, feels our heartaches, and knows our pain and our grief. He cares about our struggles, and He is able to bring us through. God is able to turn situations around, able to do what we can't do, and able to provide for our every need. He is a present help in the time of trouble. God is able to do just what He promised. Stand on His Word because His Word is true! He is a way maker and a promise keeper.

God is able in our darkest place, in our most difficult place, and in our place of indecision. One divine connection can shift you from victim to victor. Don't lose your focus

> God is able to turn situations around, able to do what we can't do, and able to provide for our every need. He is a present help in the time of trouble.

because of what it looks like now. Greater is coming! This is a season of miracles, momentum, and manifested blessings.

Bartimaeus sensed there was something going on around him. He could not see, but He *heard* the noise of the crowd. It has been proven that when someone loses one sense, the other senses become stronger, especially if that sense is lost early in life. Blind people may hear better. And hearing is important because faith comes by hearing and hearing the word of God. I'm sure the noise was louder than the normal chatter he heard because of the large crowd that was following Jesus. Bartimaeus recognized this was different and asked the people what was going on. Someone tells him that Jesus is passing by.

Bartimaeus recognized Jesus had the power and the authority to help him. Jesus was his only hope. He needed a miracle, and it was time to step up. There was anticipation and expectation in the atmosphere. He did not want to miss the moment. He decided to step up with what he had. He could not see but he had a voice. We have to use what we have. Bartimaeus began to shout out! "Jesus thou Son of David, have mercy on me!"

He sprung forward because he had the faith to believe. He had to maximize the moment as he didn't know how long Jesus was going to be nearby. This is not the season to procrastinate. Step up, step out, and step forward. If you have the faith to believe, you will receive. While you're waiting, believe. While you're crying, believe. Miracles are still happening, so believe.

The Bible says if you can believe, all things are possible. We are walking in amazing faith and we believe God for amazing blessings. It's important that our confessions line up with what God says about our lives. Confess that you are blessed and highly favored. That means jobs and better jobs, promotions and increase, supernatural debt cancellation, unexpected checks in the mail, and restoration and divine favor.

According to your faith, be it unto you! God is not just your resource, but He is your source. Everything we need is in Jesus; He never fails.

Bartimaeus had to speak up!

You have to speak up:

Speak those things that be not as though they were.

Speak positivity over that negative doctor's report.

Speak success over what failed the last time.

Speak life over that dead relationship.

Speak destiny over your children.

Speak peace in the midst of chaos and turmoil.

Speak unity where there is division.

The people around Bartimaeus tried to shut him down. They wanted to silence him. There will always be people who tell you to be quiet. They will tell you that it doesn't take all of that. Please don't let anyone shut you up when you need a breakthrough. They don't have a clue about what you really need. Sometimes, it is desperation that propels your determination. Don't focus on opinions and opposition; focus on the opportunity. Many people are so focused on opinions and people pleasing that they miss their opportunity. Every now and then, you have to cry louder like the blind man. Keep on calling on the name of Jesus, because it's Jesus who has the power to turn your situation around.

When Bartimaeus shouted out, he got Jesus's attention. Jesus stopped and called him to come from the back to the front of the line. Some of the same people that

Sometimes, it is **desperation** that propels your determination. Don't focus on opinions and opposition; **focus on the opportunity.**

were trying to block Bartimaeus's blessings had to go get him and bring him to the front of the line. There may be some people who have been blocking your blessings that will have to step aside and let you through. When it's your time and your turn, no one can hinder what God has for you.

Suddenly, the people started saying cheer up, be of good comfort, rise up, Jesus is calling for you. Bartimaeus sprung forward! He was ready to break forth! When you receive a word from Jesus, you have to step out, step up, and step forward! He got up, threw off his coat, threw off frustration, threw off disappointment, threw off hurt, threw off rejection, threw off his limitations, and came to Jesus. It's time to throw off some things to get to Jesus.

When he got in the presence of Jesus, Jesus asked him what he wanted. Jesus already knew the answer, but he wanted him to *speak* it. He didn't give any excuses for his condition or blame anyone, but straightway said that he wanted to see and receive his sight. The Bible says that because of his faith, he received his sight instantly and was made whole. Faith makes the way for blessings and opens the door for healing and breakthrough. Bartimaeus experienced his breakthrough so he could break forth into a new season.

Chapter 3
Breaking Free from the Past:
Let Go and Let God

> Now Naaman, captain of the host of the king of Syria, was a great man with his master, and honourable, because by him the Lord had given deliverance unto Syria: he was also a mighty man in valour, but he was a leper. And the Syrians had gone out by companies, and had brought away captive out of the land of Israel a little maid; and she waited on Naaman's wife. And she said unto her mistress, Would God my lord were with the prophet that is in Samaria! for he would recover him of his leprosy.
>
> **2 Kings 5:1-3 KJV**

God is concerned about every aspect of our lives. He is well able to perfect everything that concerns us. There is nothing too hard for Him. With God, all things are possible if we believe. Our belief is according to our faith. Faith is the substance of things hoped for and the evidence of things not seen. Faith is an action and faith has to be activated by action.

We have to be willing to trust Him even when we can't trace Him. This next season will demand radical faith. Radical faith believes beyond what the natural eye sees. We must walk by faith and not by sight. There has to be a willingness to release everything to God and allow Him to order our steps. We will never experience breaking forth to greater holding on to the past. We will miss the greater opportunities trying to control the smaller ones. Learn to let go and let God. What's ahead of us is greater than what's behind us. Letting go and letting God sets us up to break forth. Are you willing to release everything to Him?

In this passage, we find that Naaman was a commander of the army of the king of Syria. He was a man of status, walked in authority, and victorious in battle. Naaman walked in favor and was well respected by his superiors. From the outside, Naaman appeared to have it going on. Outward appearances can be deceiving. Naaman was dealing with his own personal inner struggles. This text paints a picture of a great man, but there is a "but" in the first verse. Whenever we see "but" it alerts us there's more to the story. Naaman was dealing with a private battle in the midst of all of his greatness.

You may think that you aren't capable, aren't qualified, or your past unqualifies you to be used. He wants to take your mess and not only bless you but use it to bless others!

In that day, leprosy was a serious skin condition infecting parts of or all the body. Lepers were shunned and considered unclean by many. We don't know the severity of Naaman's case, but we do know he was able to still function in his dysfunction. He was a great man, but he privately struggled and publicly served. Throughout the Bible, leprosy was often compared to sin. The early Israelites believed it was a punishment for sin and a curse. During those times, it was a chronic and incurable disease.

Naaman was battling an issue beyond his control. All of us have issues. Naaman was no different from you or me. We may be saved, anointed, and appointed, but the reality is we have issues. We still press our way day after day regardless of our issues. Weekly, we still serve, work, teach, and preach. There will always be obstacles, roadblocks, and hindrances on our journey to destiny.

We are a work in progress. God is molding, making, and shaping us for His glory. He is refining us to be used in a greater capacity. When He gets through with us, we shall come forth as pure gold. God desires to use all of us. You may think that you aren't capable, aren't qualified, or your past unqualifies you to be used. You are just the type of person God is looking for. He wants to take your mess and not only bless you but use it to bless others! He's only waiting on your obedience.

In this passage of scripture, we see God use a little servant girl for His divine purpose. He uses her to connect a man in need with his breakthrough blessing. The Bible does not give us her name; we only know that she was a young Israelite girl who had been captured by Naaman's army and became the servant of Naaman's wife.

The young girl had been taken from her home and brought into a strange land. She still maintained enough compassion in her heart to be sensitive to the suffering of others. Her empathy even extended to the one that was responsible for her captivity. The servant girl discerned Naaman was dealing with a monumental issue. She had monumental faith for a miracle.

This girl maximized the moment and directed him to the problem solver. She could have remained silent, but she put her faith into action. She went to Naaman's wife and told her about a prophet in Samaria by the name of Elisha. She believed if her master could connect with the prophet, God would give him a breakthrough.

You never know who God will use to be a blessing in your life. Your blessing may come through who you least expect. Can you receive from someone who isn't on your level or someone you believe is unqualified to give you a word? Would you dismiss what they say, or would you follow the instruction? This girl could have been bitter about her capture, but God's hand was on her life. She had been positioned for a purpose. God placed her in that position to be a blessing so He could get the glory!

God had already made provision for Naaman's breakthrough. Every breakthrough is not immediate; sometimes we have to go through a process to get to the breakthrough. The breakthrough precedes breaking forth. God has a way of processing us in the process. He molds us and shapes us for His glory. He clears some things out of us and inputs what is necessary. It's similar to a clearance sale. God takes inventory to assess what we are operating with. He checks to see if there is too much pride, too much envy, too much jealousy, too much flesh, too much anger, or too much disobedience. He evaluates other issues like wrong motives, hatred, lying, backbiting and more.

He takes us through a process to clear what will not be needed. When seasons change, we have to be prepared for that new season. Some of things we were holding on to in our last season won't work in our new season. Our shelves have to be restocked with what's necessary. We need more compassion, more love, more patience, more anointing, and more strength. God knows how to replenish us and restore us completely.

God had a breakthrough for Naaman, but Naaman had to go through a process. What's so amazing about God is that you never know how He is going to move. His thoughts are not our thoughts and His ways are not our ways. He may not move how or when we think He should move, but His promises always come to pass. Can you still be obedient and patient when you think the blessing is going to come just like the last time, but God has something completely different in mind this time?

What is that thing that's standing between you and your breakthrough blessing? Naaman had to shift some things to get the breakthrough to break forth. The first thing he shifted was his priority. He dropped everything on his agenda and focused on the possibility. His problem required a sense of urgency. He shifted everything to get in the presence of the One who had the power and the authority to change the situation.

The next thing Naaman shifted was his position. He was a man of status, but he had to humble himself. Humility often requires more listening than talking. The scripture says that the information Naaman needed for his healing came from a very unusual and unlikely source. The instructions came from an ordinary girl that was serving his wife. Despite being in a strange land, she never forgot her God. She never forgot the power of God and she never forgot that God is a healer; she held on to her faith.

Every now and then, we have to shift out of our comfort zone. We have to move by faith to do something we've never done. If we continue doing what we've always done, we will keep getting the same results. Naaman could

Moving to new levels and new dimensions require a shifting. You may have to **shift your prayer life** to a greater level of intimacy. You may have to shift to be more intentional in seeking Him consistently. There may be a need to turn down your plate and fast.

have continued to be miserable by accepting his life the way it was and wishing to be healed. Instead, he made the decision to step up and do something different. One right decision can shift you in the right direction for your destiny.

Shifting yields different results. Moving to new levels and new dimensions requires a shifting. You may have to shift your prayer life to a greater level of intimacy. You may have to shift to be more intentional in seeking Him consistently. There may be a need to turn down your plate and fast.

When Naaman thought things over, he came to the realization that maybe, just maybe, the God of the Israelite girl was able to heal him. He decided he was going to the king of Syria to get permission to go and see the prophet. Naaman did not delay when he received a word that help was possible. How many blessings have we missed procrastinating, waiting, and delaying? Naaman received the word and moved immediately. He had struggled too long with leprosy and was ready for a breakthrough.

The scripture says that Naaman went to his master and told him what the servant girl from Israel had spoken. His master tells him to go and even writes a letter to the king of Israel asking him to cure Naaman of leprosy. Naaman goes off to Israel with the letter. He brings gifts as well—gold, silver and clothing.

The young girl said there is a prophet in Israel but Naaman's master wrote a letter to the king of Israel. The king of Israel did not have the power or the authority to heal Naaman. When you are in need of a blessing, looking for a miracle, or waiting for a breakthrough, you have to go to the right source. The king could not do what God was about to do through the prophet.

When Elisha, the prophet, heard that the king had become angry with the request and torn his robe, he sent word to have Naaman come to him. Naaman went with all of his horses, chariots, and servants. He stopped at the door of Elisha's house. He was expecting the prophet to come out wave his hand over him, lay hands on him, or speak healing to his body personally. Elisha does not even come to greet him; instead, he sends a messenger with instructions: "Go, wash yourself seven times in the Jordan, and your flesh will be restored, and you will be cleansed."

Naaman didn't see this coming. He became upset and was insulted that he was told to dip in the dirty Jordan

River. He even names two other rivers that he thinks would be a cleaner and better choice. Sometimes God's instructions may seem ridiculous, but we have to discern the voice of the Lord. God releases blessings and breakthrough in His own time and His own way. Every now and then, we have to get ourselves out of the way. We are often the greatest hindrance to our blessings.

Naaman almost missed his blessing by being disobedient and having a bad attitude. Fortunately, he had surrounded himself with people who had his best interest at heart. It's important to be connected to people who want God's best for us. We need people who can talk us off the ledge when we are about to make a mistake. Naaman's servants encouraged him to think about it again. They said, "If the prophet had told you to do some great thing, would you not have done it? How much more, then, when he tells you, 'Wash and be cleansed!'"

It's important to be connected to people who want God's best for us. We need people who can talk us off the ledge when we are about to make a mistake.

Naaman was at the point where he didn't have any other options. Reluctantly, he went down to the river and stepped off the banks of the Jordan. He followed Elisha's instructions and dipped in the river seven times. He was cleaned like a young boy when he came out. Naaman had to let go and let God! He let go of his pride and his rage. He released the things hindering his breakthrough and limiting him breaking forth. There are times when we have to let go of past hurt, shame, and guilt. It's time to let go of pain, unforgiveness, and disappointments. Let go and let God be God!

If we can believe, all things are possible. Naaman's obedience to God's directions led to his breakthrough. God allowed him to breakthrough the issue and break forth into his greater destiny.

Chapter 4
Breaking Through the Obstacles: The Giants Must Come Down

> And David said to Saul, Let no man's heart fail because of him; thy servant will go and fight with this Philistine. And Saul said to David, Thou art not able to go against this Philistine to fight with him: for thou art but a youth, and he a man of war from his youth. And David said unto Saul, Thy servant kept his father's sheep, and there came a lion, and a bear, and took a lamb out of the flock: And I went out after him, and smote him, and delivered it out of his mouth: and when he arose against me, I caught him by his beard, and smote him, and slew him. Thy servant slew both the lion and the bear: and this uncircumcised Philistine shall be as one of them, seeing he hath defied the armies of the living God. David said moreover, The Lord that delivered me out of the paw of the lion, and out of the paw of the bear, he will deliver me out of the hand of this Philistine. And Saul said unto David, Go, and the Lord be with thee.
>
> **1 Samuel 17:32-37**

The journey to breaking forth to greater requires breakthrough obstacles. Obstacles block our way and hinder our success. They delay us and detour us on the way to our destiny. Obstacles are often unavoidable, but they have purpose. Obstacles and opposition challenge us and strengthen our faith. The opposition is not sent to destroy us but to develop us.

All of us have to battle one giant or another. Giants are those obstacles or problems that seem impossible to overcome. Often, we make the giants more important than they really are. There is a tendency to make small problems seem gigantic. We can make the mistake of magnifying the power of the enemy in our minds. Way too much credit is given to our adversary. The enemy attempts to convince us that we are powerless. He always speaks contrary to the will of God. God's Word reminds us of the power and authority He has given to us. We may be broken in the battle, but we will not be denied the breakthrough. We are a victorious people and giants are already defeated. The battle is not ours it is the Lord's. We are not victims, but we are victorious!

I declare to you God is in control of everything that's going on in our lives and in the world. God can handle our giants. It doesn't matter what we're facing—our God is greater and stronger. He's bigger than anything we are going through! There will be times when our faith will be tested. How will you handle the giants? Are you going to crumble under the pressure or trust God for the breakthrough like David?

Every day we face some kind of challenge. Challenges on the job, challenges to finish school, challenges to walk in our assignment, health challenges, relationship challenges, financial challenges, challenges for peace, and even challenges to live a life pleasing to God. Then there are giants we battle internally. We battle silent giants like low self-esteem, depression, fear, anger, abuse, or addiction. The constant pressure elevates our anxiety level. We can become frustrated and overwhelmed because the struggle is real.

God is greater than our greatest struggle. His power overrides every obstacle and gives us the victory. We are more than conquerors. We are winning in spite of every obstacle. Victorious people must maintain a victorious mindset. Victory belongs to us! All giants do fall.

God has a plan to defeat every giant we face. Trust His plan and His process. Be patient and wait on Him to conquer the giants. He will give you divine strategies and the power to succeed. Do not be discouraged because things don't happen when you think they should. Every blessing and breakthrough is not instantaneous. God's timing is the best timing. God wants to deal with our giants and give us victory.

We are a victorious people and giants are already defeated. The battle is not ours it is the Lord's. We are not victims, but we are victorious!

In 1 Samuel 17:1-10, we find a battle is about to take place.

"Now the Philistines gathered together their armies to battle, and were gathered together at Shochoh, which belongeth to Judah, and pitched between Shochoh and Azekah, in Ephesdammim. And Saul and the men of Israel were gathered together, and pitched by the valley of Elah, and set the battle in array against the Philistines. And the Philistines stood on a mountain on the one side, and Israel stood on a mountain on the other side: and there was a valley between them. And there went out a champion out of the camp of the Philistines, named Goliath, of Gath, whose height was six cubits and a span. And he had a helmet of brass upon his head, and he was armed with a coat of mail; and the weight of the coat was five thousand shekels of brass. And he had greaves of brass upon his legs, and a target of brass between his shoulders. And the staff of his spear was like a weaver's beam; and his spear's head weighed six hundred shekels of iron: and one bearing a shield went before him. And he stood and cried unto the armies of Israel, and said unto them, why are ye come out to set your battle in array? am not I a Philistine, and ye servants to Saul? choose you a man for you and let him come down to me. If he be able to fight with me, and to kill me, then will we be your servants: but if I prevail against him, and kill him, then shall ye be our servants, and serve us. And the Philistine said, I defy the armies of Israel this day; give me a man, that we may fight together. When Saul and all Israel heard those words of the Philistine, they were dismayed, and greatly afraid."

The enemy will always mess with our minds first. If he can get in our head and make us afraid, he has already won half the battle. Do not be intimidated by the noise of the enemy. When the enemy whispers in your ear, counter his voice with the Word of God!

David, the shepherd boy, was sent by his father to check on his brothers who were in Saul's army. As he approached, he heard the battle cry, and he ran to the front lines to see what was happening. He heard the challenge of Goliath.

"And David spake to the men that stood by him, saying, What shall be done to the man that killeth this Philistine, and taketh away the reproach from Israel? for who is this uncircumcised Philistine, that he should defy the armies of the living God?" (v. 26)

Saul's men were focused on the problem—they saw a giant they couldn't handle. All they could see was defeat, but David's focus was on the problem solver. You have to develop a victorious perspective. You must see yourself winning even when the problem seems insurmountable. In order to break forth, you must stay focused and maintain the right perspective. We don't have to be afraid of the giant. The giant in us has power over every other giant.

David let faith overshadow any fear he had. He had a heart for God, but David also had the heart of a warrior. In this season, God is looking for faith warriors. This is not the season to wimp out! David realized that the real battle belonged to the Lord! He was absolutely convinced that it was God's plan for the giants to fall; they cannot stand. We must be confident in the power and the presence of God. No obstacle is too hard for God to overcome.

David handled the giant by facing it. He didn't run away from him but moved towards him. It is imperative we remember that we cannot conquer what we are unwilling to confront. There are some habits and bad connections/relationships that won't be broken until we deal with them head on.

> We don't have to be afraid of the giant. The giant in us has power over every other giant.

Do not be intimidated by the noise of the enemy. When the enemy whispers in your ear, counter his voice with the Word of God!

David volunteered for the assignment. God had already prepared him in the wilderness when he slew the lion and bear. Keep this in mind: before David faced the giant, he was being prepared in the wilderness. He was the shepherd boy tending to the sheep. Often, we don't understand why God may have us doing something that we deem insignificant. Don't despise it. Learn all that you can; He just may be preparing you for your giant.

When David decided to face the giant, he encountered doubt and negativity. Eliab, David's oldest brother, heard David speaking with the men and became angry. He questioned him about who were tending the sheep. Eliab, believing that David is just conceited, thinks he only came down to watch the battle. When you step forward to do something for God, be prepared for opposition. Those closest to you may not truly believe in you. But you can't listen to their voice. Recognize God has prepared you to complete the assignment.

Sometimes being anointed attracts jealousy. The anointing comes with a price. There are times we may be misunderstood and our motives misjudged. The enemy will try to silence us and make us think our assignment is insignificant or that we can't complete it. Don't allow other people's insecurity to impact your destiny. You're anointed for this!

We have to stand on who we are and whose we are. Breaking forth to greater requires us to walk in who God called us to be. If God said we can do it, then we can. Obstacles are just an opportunity for God to get the glory.

There will always be people who will not acknowledge your value. Saul wanted to focus on David's inability instead of his ability. He suggested he was not qualified to go up

> Sometimes being anointed attracts jealousy. Don't allow other people's insecurity to impact your destiny. You're anointed for this!

against this giant. He reminded him that he was just a youth and that Goliath had been fighting from a youth. However, if we are going to face our giants, we have to focus on God's ability and not our inability. God doesn't call the equipped, but He equips those He calls. He empowers us to do more with Him than we could without Him. There is no limit with God. Often, we limit Him with our limited thinking. We should strive to take the limits off our thinking. God is able to do exceedingly abundantly above what we ask or think. Breaking forth to greater requires living with expectation. Believers have to expect something greater, expect something new, expect the extraordinary.

It is important to reflect on God's victories in the past when we are facing giants. David reminded Saul that when he came upon the roaring the lion, God gave him the victory and he overcame it. When the bear came, God gave him the victory, and he overcame that, too. Sometimes we have to deal with the lions and bears before we get to the giants. Lions and bears are those things that try to kill, steal, and destroy our destiny. David believed that if God gave him victory then, He's going to give me victory now. God has a

It is imperative that we remember that we cannot **conquer what we are unwilling to confront.** There are some habits and bad connections/relationships that won't be broken *until we deal with them head on.*

proven track record, and we don't have to look far to see His hand at work. If you are facing something big, just think on something He has already done. He is the same yesterday, today, and forevermore. You don't have to wait until the battle is over; you can shout now. You're coming out with victory.

David learned to lean and depend on God through his experiences in the wilderness. He developed the habit of relying on the power and presence of God. His level of intimacy with God grew with every experience. We must come to a place in our spiritual walk where we trust God beyond what we see. Our faith has to supersede our fear. Real faith believes even when we don't see the possibility.

There isn't a giant God cannot handle. He is greater than every giant we will face. Nothing is impossible to overcome with God. Every obstacle is just an opportunity for God to show Himself mighty. Every giant must fall!

Chapter 5
Breaking into Deeper:
Take the Limits Off

> And it came to pass, that, as the people pressed upon him to hear the word of God, he stood by the lake of Gennesaret, And saw two ships standing by the lake: but the fishermen were gone out of them, and were washing their nets. And he entered into one of the ships, which was Simon's, and prayed him that he would thrust out a little from the land. And he sat down, and taught the people out of the ship. Now when he had left speaking, he said unto Simon, Launch out into the deep, and let down your nets for a draught. And Simon answering said unto him, Master, we have toiled all the night, and have taken nothing: nevertheless at thy word I will let down the net.
> **Luke 5:1-5 KJV**

Often, we cannot move into unlimited possibilities because our thinking is limited. Our thinking can paralyze us into inactivity. Some of our thinking causes us to be in a stuck position—stuck in the same place, with the same dead job, doing the same things, dealing with the same drama, emotions, and fears. It's time to take the limits off our thinking! God has greater in store for you!

In this scripture, we find Jesus down by the Lake of Gennesaret which is also known as the Sea of Galilee. Jesus is teaching the Word of God under the anointing with power and authority. The Bible lets us know that the crowds are following after Him. When Jesus moves, they move. They are hanging onto every Word that comes out of His mouth. They are seeking something He has. They are seeking to be in His presence and are hungry for the Word of God. The amazing thing about hunger is that it is a driving force. It will drive us to make a decision to satisfy our appetites. We will either make a decision for the things of God or the things of the world. We have a choice!

Have you ever had a hunger pang but didn't know what you wanted to eat? You had a taste for Ruth's Chris Steakhouse but settled for a local fast-food restaurant because it was convenient, closer, and cheaper. It stopped the pang, but it didn't really satisfy you. It was just a temporary fix!

Many people are emotionally hungry. Hungry for success, hungry for attention, hungry for affirmation, hungry for affection, and hungry for love. Our hunger can drive us to look for satisfaction and fulfillment in all the wrong places. I

When Jesus steps into your boat, into your situation, into your life, **anything** can happen!

pose the question: what is it that you are really seeking?

May I suggest that many of us are spiritually hungry and don't recognize what's missing. There are voids and empty places in our lives that we keep trying to satisfy with a temporary fix. A new relationship, new outfit, new shoes, or even a new place won't do it. What we are missing is a deeper relationship with God. It's time to go deeper. Jesus is the answer. He has the power to satisfy every need we have.

In this passage of scripture, as Jesus is walking, He sees two empty boats. The fishermen are done for the day. They have gone to wash and mend their nets. Jesus steps aboard one of the boats that belongs to Simon Peter. It was not by accident but by divine design He steps into Simon Peter's boat. When Jesus steps into your boat, into your situation, into your life, anything can happen! He tells Simon Peter to push away from the shore a little. Simon Peter is obedient and pushes out. Jesus continues to teach the people from the boat. When He finishes, He gives Simon Peter some instructions. He tells him to launch out into the deep.

To *launch* means to thrust; to set in motion! It means to go beyond or to stretch beyond your limits. It's time to move from the shallow water to the deeper water; move from the comfortable to the uncomfortable; move from the familiar to the unfamiliar.

Jesus was telling Simon Peter to go back—go back to some of the same territory you've already been over. Go back to the place where you didn't have success the first time, but this time, go out deeper. God will shift your present location to reposition you to the right destination for the blessing. Simon Peter was by the shore, but his blessing was in the deep waters. The Word compelled him to launch out into the deep. There are some things in the depths of the ocean that we can't see hanging out on the shore.

Jesus says to Simon Peter to let down his net for a big catch. He sets up an expectation. Jesus is about to exceed Simon's expectations. Simon Peter doesn't expect anything to happen as he and the other fishermen had toiled all night and not caught anything.

God will reposition you to give you a greater revelation. What God wants you to experience cannot be experienced in a shallow place. Your prayer life, commitment, discipline, and worship must go deeper to experience all God has for you. You must go deeper and develop an intimate

> # God will shift your present location to reposition you to the right destination for the blessing.

relationship with God. Go deeper to see greater, to receive your healing, to be healed from everywhere you hurt.

No longer can we make excuses. Blame, denial, and making excuses are destiny distractions. We just have to move by faith. Simon's initial response was an excuse: he's an expert fisherman and had been fishing all night, but the fish were not biting. He has every reason to be frustrated but he does not allow his frustration to override his faith. Frustration will cause you to run, miss your blessing, or miss a divine connection. Your faith has to be greater than your frustration. So, Simon Peter listens to the voice of Jesus and obeys His instruction.

The blessing is always connected to obedience. Obedience will position you for overflow blessings. When Simon Peter obeyed Jesus, that's when the blessing showed up. The Bible says that when they launched their net in the deep waters, they caught a great number of fish. They caught so many fish that their net began to break. The blessing was so great that they had to call for backup. They signaled to their partners in the other boat to come and help them.

Not only was one boat filled, but both boats were so filled to capacity that they began to sink. Simon Peter's obedience was the catalyst for his blessing, but others were blessed as well. Your family is going to be blessed by your obedience. Your business will be blessed by your obedience. Your ministry will blossom because of obedience. Everything and everyone attached to you will be blessed.

Simon Peter had an encounter that renewed his mind. He was operating in the natural, but he experienced the supernatural. Acceleration showed up. God gave to them in a matter of minutes what would have taken them all night and all day to catch. The Lord spoke a word and increase showed up. Everyone was amazed at what the Lord had done. Simon was so amazed that it caused him to fall down at Jesus's knees and pronounce that he was a sinful man. Jesus gave him a supernatural demonstration of power and authority that Simon Peter might believe. Jesus was preparing him to break forth to his destiny. There was a greater assignment on

> # The blessing is always connected to obedience. Obedience will position you for overflow blessings.

Simon Peter's life than just being a fisherman. God changed his assignment and made him a fisher of men. Christ was going to use him to save souls. God is preparing you and processing you for a greater purpose. Take the limits off your thinking! If you will be like Simon Peter and launch out on faith, you will see God perform great and mighty acts in your life.

Chapter 6
Breaking Forth into Greater: Quitting is Not an Option

> And a certain woman, which had an issue of blood twelve years, And had suffered many things of many physicians, and had spent all that she had, and was nothing bettered, but rather grew worse, When she had heard of Jesus, came in the press behind, and touched his garment. For she said, If I may touch but his clothes, I shall be whole. And straightway the fountain of her blood was dried up; and she felt in her body that she was healed of that plague. And Jesus, immediately knowing in himself that virtue had gone out of him, turned him about in the press, and said, Who touched my clothes? And his disciples said unto him, Thou seest the multitude thronging thee, and sayest thou, Who touched me? And he looked round about to see her that had done this thing. But the woman fearing and trembling, knowing what was done in her, came and fell down before him, and told him all the truth. And he said unto her, Daughter, thy faith hath made thee whole; go in peace, and be whole of thy plague.

Perseverance is essential on our journey to breaking forth to greater. The journey will consist of both mountaintop and valley experiences. There are times we will be frustrated and overwhelmed. Some seasons will cause us to become discouraged enough to want to give up. Finishing strong is not an option if we quit in the middle. Many times, we are tempted to give up just before the breakthrough. Our success is within reach, but we miss the moment because we become weary. We must continue to strive despite difficulties. Quitting is not an option.

We are introduced to three difficult situations in this text. The situations are different, but the solution to the problem is the same! We find the deliverance of the demon-possessed man, there is the healing of a woman who has been suffering with an issue of sickness for twelve years, and there is the raising of Jarius's daughter from the dead. Each one of these situations gives us a greater revelation of Jesus. In this chapter, we see Him as the deliverer, we see Him as the healer, and we see Him as the great resurrector!

The man, the woman, and the girl all experienced a miraculous breakthrough. Miracles were happening everywhere Jesus showed up! There are moments in our lives when we need an answered prayer or blessing. There are other times when only a miracle will suffice. We come to the realization that the problem will not be solved unless God intervenes. If God does not show up or if He does not turn the circumstances around, then it will not get done. He is the great miracle worker, and miracles are still possible.

Well, what is a miracle? A *miracle* is the manifestation of something extraordinary. It is something unusual, something phenomenal. It is when God Himself places His super on a natural situation and causes a supernatural experience. You are a miracle. You have family and friends that are walking, talking miracles. The situation seemed dreadful, but then God stepped in and gave them a miraculous breakthrough. They didn't just survive, they overcame. It's a miracle they are even still here.

Someone can testify about how God stepped into their situation and turned it around. They can testify God gave them a breakthrough from sickness, suffering, pain, shame, and guilt of the past. It was God who allowed us to survive the loss of people, places, and possessions. We didn't survive but we overcame. Now we are in a position to break forth to our greater.

Jesus used the demonstration of miracles for various reasons. Each miracle had a purpose. One of the purposes miracles served was to help the unbeliever believe. There

You don't have to give up or give in. There is **power available for your breakthrough** so you can break forth to all God has for you. Quitting is not an option!

are some people who don't believe anything until they've seen it for themselves. The miracles demonstrated Jesus's power and compassion. He also often used miracles to affirm His identity.

His power heals us physically from all infirmities and all manner of disease. His power can heal us emotionally from a wounded heart. His miracle-working power heals us from the pain of the past. He can heal us from the hurt of those things people did to us that they should not have done.

His power can heal us everywhere our heart is hurting. His power heals us spiritually; it can heal us from rejection. He has the power to deliver us from every addiction and bad habit. His power can release us and heal us from toxic relationships. Jesus can deliver us from verbal, physical, sexual, and emotional abuse. We don't have to remain bound. God wants to break every chain holding us and set us free!

He gives us the power to keep pressing forth. He gives us the power to persevere. His power is a yoke-destroying power—the kind of power that breaks chains: the chains on our minds and the chains that keep us in a complacent place. His-miracle working power is able to heal us from the

> **We may have some issues, but our issues don't have to have us. God is greater than our issues.**

strongholds on our minds. It can heal us from anger, aggression, depression, oppression, and all mental illness. We can be set free. You don't have to give up or give in. There is power available for your breakthrough so you can break forth to all God has for you. Quitting is not an option!

There's nothing you are in that God cannot bring you out of. The depth of your pain is no obstacle for God. He specializes in going into the deep and secret places to set us free. It is His will that we are free to be who He destined us to be.

There are issues in our lives. As a matter of fact, issues are part of our journey. The reality is that we all face real issues. We are challenged by real family issues, financial issues, relationship issues, job issues, health issues, emotional issues, and flesh issues. Often, people applaud our public success but are oblivious to our private struggles and issues. We may have some issues, but our issues don't have to have us. God is greater than our issues.

The woman in this scripture had been struggling from this blood issue for twelve long years. Twelve years is a long season to be going through anything, especially something so crippling. She had been separated and isolated from her family and her friends because of the nature of her condition. In that day, if you had any kind of blood issue, you couldn't go into the synagogue, because you were considered ceremonially unclean. So, this woman is no stranger to rejection. She knew what it's like to be abandoned. Picture yourself in her situation. A situation that should have been short term turns into twelve long years. You can't go to the church for refuge. You can't go to friends or family or depend on anyone you trust. You are isolated from everything you know to be familiar. What do you do?

She had spent all the money she had going from doctor to doctor. Whenever it seems like things are beginning to turn around, they get worse. There doesn't seem to be a solution, but quitting is not an option.

Can you imagine her desperation? You may be able to identify with her because for many years, you've been praying for your son or daughter or that wayward grandchild. You begin to see some progress, and then a few weeks later, they've taken a few steps backward. Or maybe you've been praying for your finances. You pay off one bill and then something unexpected happens that takes all the savings you had.

What do you do when you keep on praying, keep on worshiping, and you keep on coming to church and it looks like it's getting worse than better? What do you do when quitting is not an option? You hold on!

You're right on the edge. A breaking forth to something greater than your struggle is just around the corner. God is setting you up to be blessed, setting you up for your breakthrough, and setting you up to break forth! This woman was broken, busted, and disgusted. She was in a desperate place but she was still determined. She refused to give up because she understood quitting was not an option.

Quitting is not an option for you either. No matter how grim the situation looks, you must stay in the fight. You have to keep pressing, because pressing leads to your breakthrough, and your breakthrough leads to you breaking forth to your destiny. The woman in the text had every right to give up but she refused. Hope would not allow her to give up.

Your determination must be greater than your desperation. No matter how dire your situation looks, don't be afraid. Fear has no power over you. You cannot allow fear of failure cause you to give up. Don't miss your moment because of fear. God has not given us a spirit of fear but of power, love, and a sound mind. Quitting is not an option. Stay in the race!

The Bible says that she heard of Jesus, just like Bartimaeus. She heard that Jesus was passing by—the miracle worker, the healer, the deliverer, the present help, and the way maker, was passing her way. She made the decision that she must maximize this moment and make a divine connection. This opportunity may never pass her way again. The right decision at the right time shifts destiny in your direction. She decided to press pass every hindrance. She had grown comfortable hiding out behind closed doors for

No matter how grim the situation looks, you must stay in the fight.

twelve years, but she decided to shift her position and do something different.

You may be familiar with the saying that doing the same thing over and over and expecting different results is the definition of insane. This woman kept trying doctor after doctor and was getting the same results. It was time to make a different decision. Look at your life's issues. What issues have you been wrestling with continuously and not getting the results you want? Maybe it's time to be like this woman in the text and do something different and daring.

The Bible lets us know this woman shifted her position out of her comfort zone. She pressed her way through the crowd of people. It was a struggle, but she was determined not to give up. She crouched down and pressed forward. Quitting was not an option.

There are three key things we must consider if we're going to break forth to something new or great: You must see the possibility, put your faith into action, and speak life to your situation

1. See the Possibility: We have to see beyond our present situation. Faith allows us to believe what our eyes cannot see. We have to see ourselves blessed, healed, prosperous, joyful, restored, promoted, in a healthy marriage. We have to see ourselves walking in our calling, ministry assignment, or walking across the stage earning that degree. She stepped out of her comfort zone because she believed that breakthrough was possible. She saw it by faith and then moved based upon what she saw.

2. **Put Your Faith into Action**: She activated her faith by deciding to do something. The Bible lets us know that faith without works (action) is dead. You can declare you believe, but it's not until you step out and move that faith is activated. How do you put your faith into action? You stand on God's word and what He says about your situation. Have you received a bad doctor's report? Well, what does the word of God say about this? It says by His stripes you are healed. So, despite what the doctor said or even your feelings and emotions, stand on the word that you are healed!

3. **Speak Life to Your Situation**: Your words matter, and they have power. The Bible declares that death and life are in the power of the tongue. What are

you speaking over your life, your health, your marriage, your children, your business, your purpose, your destiny? Strive to speak more positively than negatively and watch your life change for the better. The woman with the issue of blood declared that she would be made whole if she could just touch the hem of Jesus's garment. There was no wavering; she spoke life to her destiny!

We have to speak positively to our possibility. We have to declare the salvation of our children, the prosperity of our businesses, the wholeness of our health, or the peace of our marriages. Declare our homes are blessed, we are walking in divine favor, and that we have the joy of the Lord as we fulfill our purpose. We have to speak what we desire to see.

The Bible states that straightway, immediately, the blood dried up. This woman was healed and received her breakthrough. She felt something on the inside—a breaking forth—that she was healed of the plague even before Jesus spoke to her. All it took was a touch, and she was made whole. She saw the possibility, put her faith into action, and spoke life to her situation. God can and will do the same thing for you.

Jesus recognized that power had been released from out of Him. He turned around and questioned who touched Him. Among the throng of people clamoring about Him, He recognized one touch was that of great faith. What does Jesus say about your faith? Is your faith wavering and shaky, or do you have faith like this woman that will touch Jesus and garner His attention?

The disciples didn't understand what was going on, but Jesus turned around and He didn't stop until He found her in the midst of the crowd. I declare that your faith will touch Jesus. He will touch your issue. He'll turn your issue all around.

He'll make some things brand new. He'll restore some things. He'll renew some things. This woman was fearful and trembling, but she felt the power of the breakthrough. You cannot have a real encounter with Jesus and still be the same. You cannot have an encounter with Jesus and things not change. She came and fell at His feet and told Him all the truth. She began to tell her story. She began to tell Him everything that she had been carrying and everything that was bottled up for the last twelve years. She began to

> **You cannot have a real encounter with Jesus and still be the same. You cannot have an encounter with Jesus and things not change.**

release it all to the Master. Sometimes you have to release something in order to receive something else. Transparency often proceeds transformation. When you release, you can receive all that Christ has for you.

The truth will set you free. It will free you from your past, pain, bondage, and secrets. The Bible says that after she poured out her heart and told Jesus everything, He declared that her faith made her whole, and told her to go in peace. You may have stayed awake last night with the weight of your situation on your shoulders, you may be reading this book burdened down from life's situations, or you may be troubled in your spirit. I speak peace to you and your situation. This is the kind of peace that surpasses all understanding. This is the kind of peace that the world and all it offers cannot give you.

Jesus told her that her issue was over. Your issue is over because you have the faith to believe. You have the faith to press forward and make a divine connection. This woman was made whole because she did not quit. She received the breakthrough and was able to break forth. Don't you dare quit, you are too close to breaking forth!

She could now go to those places she was barred from for the past twelve years. She could now visit those family members and friends that she couldn't be around for the last twelve years. Breakthrough had hit her entire life! This same power is available for you. You cannot stop now. You cannot give up now. There's so much more in store for you. Use your faith to change your life because quitting is not an option!

Conclusion

Breaking forth to our greatest potential is possible. All things are possible with God's help. There is nothing too hard for Him. Don't doubt the possibility that greater is an option for your life. It doesn't matter what your present condition is. God can meet you right where you are. Your history does not dictate your future destination. God's power and presence shift situations and circumstances. He can use every chapter in your story to get the glory. That includes the good, the bad, and the ugly. All of the heartache, pain, and disappointment you encountered along the way had purpose. It built something greater in you. You are in a stronger, wiser, and better positioned to break forth.

We are all a work in process striving to make progress. Breaking forth to greater is a process. Process consist of intentional steps to achieve a specific end. We must become more intentional as we embrace breaking into greater purpose. Intentional investments of time, efforts, and resources are essential. A purpose-driven life is a focused life that yields greater productivity. Your greatness is not limited by age, status, or your background.

There will be times when our progress is hindered by distractions. Distractions only come to defocus and discourage us. The enemy uses all kinds of tools to detour us on the way to our destiny. He uses fear, intimidation, complacency, low self-esteem, rejection, and other tricks to keep us in the box. God has given us power over every distraction. You don't have to stay stuck. God has made a way of escape. You can break out of the box!

Many people struggle to move forward because they are bound by the past. The past is the past. It's over, it's history, and it cannot be changed. At best, lessons are learned from the mistakes of the past. Failures are not life sentences but life lessons. Often, failure is a turning point that shifts our direction. God desires to release you from the past and set you free. What's ahead of you is greater than what's behind you.

Conclusion

Breaking free from the past releases you to pursue greater. God gives us the power to break through every obstacle. Greater is He that's in us than He that's in the world. You are not just a conqueror but more than a conqueror. There's a winner in you and you are an overcomer. You are already positioned to win.

Breaking into a deeper relationship with God is what He desires of us. A greater level of intimacy allows us to hear His voice with clarity. His voice provides divine instructions and clear instructions. Breaking into the deeper is the catalyst for breaking forth to greater.

It's imperative we keep a right perspective. Perspective encompasses the right point of view and the right attitude. It has often been said that attitude determines altitude. A positive and optimistic attitude shifts our perspective. There must be an innate belief that overcoming and succeeding are possible. Our beliefs drive our actions. If we do not have the faith to believe, we are defeated before we even get started. Our belief must be undergirded by our faith. Faith believes beyond what we see in the here and now. Faith reminds us that obstacles are just an opportunity for God to get the glory.

Every challenge, every set back, and every hindrance grows our faith to another level. Many of the things we perceive as working against us are really working for us. All things work together for good to them that believe and are called according to His purpose.

His purpose is where our focus should be directed. By faith, we embrace what seems impossible. By faith, we step into unchartered territories trusting God to navigate the way. By faith, we break forth from our present to our greater. Your greater is waiting to break forth!

About the Author

Reverend Dr. Brennetta C. Williams is the Visionary Founder and Senior Pastor of the Impact Worship Center Int'l located in Chesapeake, Virginia. The Impact Worship Center is a church with a vision to impact lives for victorious living through Christ. IWCI is committed to serving those in need and reaching the lost at any cost.

Dr. Williams received her undergraduate studies degree in Business Management from Old Dominion University in Norfolk, Virginia. After achieving her Bachelor of Science degree, she earned a Master of Divinity from the Samuel Dewitt Proctor School of Theology in Richmond, Virginia. She earned her Doctorate in Ministry from United Theological Seminary in Dayton, Ohio. Her professional background includes marketing for several leading pharmaceutical companies. Over the last decade, she has dedicated her life to providing medicines, education and community services to those affected and infected with HIV/AIDS. The experience has been instrumental in sensitizing her to the suffering of others.

Dr. Williams has been blessed to minister locally, nationally and internationally. She is passionate concerning foreign missions. Dr. Williams has served on Africa crusade teams to Tanzania, Zambia, Zimbabwe, Capetown, Durban, Mauritius, Soweto and Johannesburg, South Africa, as well as, China and Thailand. Mostly recently, she led an Operation

Impact Missions and Ministry Team to Nairobi, Kenya.

Dr. Williams answered the call to the gospel ministry and was licensed in 2003. She has served as an Associate Minister, Adjutant, Director of Prayer Ministries and in a multiplicity of capacities ministering to congregational spiritual needs.

Dr. Williams is currently affiliated with the Worship Center Worldwide Fellowship of Churches and was ordained under the spiritual covering of Bishop Millicent Hunter. She is an evangelist, conference speaker, and community advocate dedicated to faithfully serving others. Her greatest passion is working in the Kingdom of God to see lives renewed, restored and revived. She is the recipient of numerous community service awards including the 2018 MLK Missions and Ministry Award, 2019 Women of the Word and the 2020 African American Creative Community Award. Annually, Dr. Williams has hosted the Destined2Impact Empowerment Conference at the Virginia Beach Oceanfront.

Reverend Dr. Brennetta Williams is the visionary and CEO of Positive Impact Outreach Inc. This non-profit organization is dedicated to positively impacting lives of those in need through the love of Christ. Positive Impact seeks to provide assistance and needed services to the elderly, women, homeless, disadvantaged youth.

Dr. Williams is a native of South Boston, Virginia and currently resides in Chesapeake, Virginia with her husband and daughter.

www.ingramcontent.com/pod-product-compliance
Lightning Source LLC
Chambersburg PA
CBHW071022080526
44587CB00015B/2462